That Damned Fly

A LIFE IN VERSE

Gary Powell

Copyright © 2024 Gary Powell

The moral right of the author has been asserted.

Apart from any fair dealing for the purposes of research or private study, or criticism or review, as permitted under the Copyright, Designs and Patents Act 1988, this publication may only be reproduced, stored or transmitted, in any form or by any means, with the prior permission in writing of the publishers, or in the case of reprographic reproduction in accordance with the terms of licences issued by the Copyright Licensing Agency. Enquiries concerning reproduction outside those terms should be sent to the publishers.

Troubador Publishing Ltd
Unit E2 Airfield Business Park
Harrison Road, Market Harborough
Leicestershire LE16 7UL
Tel: 0116 279 2299
Email: books@troubador.co.uk
Web: www.troubador.co.uk

ISBN 978 1 80514 390 1

British Library Cataloguing in Publication Data.
A catalogue record for this book is available from the British Library.

Printed by TJ Books Ltd, Padstow, UK
Typeset in 11pt Minion Pro by Troubador Publishing Ltd, Leicester, UK

To Mum.
Always in our thoughts.
Gary, Ray and Shaun.

Poems

That Damned Fly	7
Blame the Caddy	13
Tug of War	16
The Thin Blue Line	19
A Hot Summer's Night (1978)	22
What a Waste	24
The Football Match	27
The Thieves	30
116 Baker Street	32
My Loyal Friend	35
A Journey on the Central Line	38
The Brixton Bomb	42
Squares of London	47
The Four Corners of St James's Square	49
The London Plane	51
The Monument	52
The Ash Cloud	54

The Bookshop	56
I'm a Papyrophiliac	57
A Nation's Cathedral	59
A Relationship That Hasn't Always Been So Special	61
Mum	63
Thankful	65
September	68
Let the Train Take the Strain	70
The Taxman (or Woman)	72
A Drive in London	75
The Greasy Spoon	78
Two Ladies Fighting	81
My Local	83
Man's Best Friend	85
There's a Bank – Where?	87
A True English Gent	89
That's a Ripper	91
The Shameless Phallus	93
Us British	95
The English National Anthem	98
The Local Council	100
Cows in a Field	101
The Granny Flat	102
The Bowling Green	103
The Future	104

That Damned Fly

In my bedroom I have a fly, it won't die. I don't know why!
A rolled-up mag,
Some Blu-tack affixed to a very long stick,
Whatever I use just doesn't do the trick.

In my bedroom I have a fly, it won't die. I don't know why!
It dodges my swipes with a deft stealth,
I haven't slept for so many nights,
It's just not good for my health.

In my bedroom I have a fly, it won't die. I don't know why!
It buzzes around during the hours of light,
And dive-bombs me in the middle of the night.
I've negotiated with the resident spider,
To entrap it in its silky web,
Promising it, if successful,
It will have a home until January or Feb.

In my bedroom I have a fly, it won't die. I don't know why!
I used a can of premium fly spray,
Which I thought would be up to the task,
It's still flying about even though I pray,
It must own a ruddy mask.

In my bedroom I have a fly, it won't die. I don't know why!
A decent night's sleep I now badly lack,
I daren't roll over and sleep on my back,
As I'm scared it will be tempted to explore,
My open mouth when I loudly snore.

In my bedroom I have a fly, it won't die. I don't know why!
It avoids the open windows; it hangs out in the nets.
It must have three-sixty radar,
As I only get so far,
Before it flexes his spindly legs,
And flaps his scaly wings,
Flies towards the lampshade,
It is running me round in rings.

In my bedroom I have a fly, it won't die. I don't know why!
Its life cycle eventually comes to an end,
At last!
He's been driving me around the bend.
Even though it caused me to shout and spit,
I have developed a certain respect for it.

In my bedroom I have a fly,
I no longer have that dread,
It's DEAD!

From Cradle to Blue Serge

Kenton is a small suburb of Greater London which, up until 1965, came under the administrative control of the historic County of Middlesex. It can be found languishing at the top end of London Underground's Bakerloo line and less than a mile from Wembley Stadium, whose twin towers were once visible on a clear day. The whole area is now overshadowed by the unattractive Northwick Park Hospital designed in the sixties and opened by the late Queen Elizabeth II in 1970.

I was born in July 1959 in the front bedroom of my maternal grandparents' rented house in a small cul-de-sac: No. 6 Vine Court. My mother and father moved into my grandparents' house for my birth, not an unusual occurrence in those days. My parents had been living with my paternal grandparents in a small two-bedroomed flat above a Chinese takeaway and a dentist: No. 196A Burnt Oak Broadway. When Mum fell pregnant, the decision was made – probably by my grandmothers – that it would be best for her to have the baby in Kenton; I doubt the mother-to-be had much say in the matter.

Following my birth, we stayed in Kenton for a couple of months before moving back to Burnt Oak Broadway with my paternal grandparents. The return was mainly for work purposes. Dad and Grandad both worked in the Frigidaire assembly plant in Colindale a mile or so south on the Edgware Road. Mum got a job in a factory in nearby South Road, as a typist. Life was pretty hard for them both, and they desperately needed a place of their own.

Sometime later, they were offered a rental property in South Road, No. 12a. It was a three-bedroomed first-floor maisonette at a rental rate they could just about afford. My memories of 12a are pretty dismal. The front main bedroom was uninhabitable through damp. The walls were always wet and the room smelled of decay.

The two remaining bedrooms – my parents' room and the one that I shared with my brother Ray – were *just* habitable. The back garden was overgrown and still had an Anderson shelter from the Second World War. The area was like an adventure playground for my brother and I. Much of the area comprised of wasteland and derelict buildings, damaged during air raids, to explore.

On the corner of South Road was a pub called the Royal Oak. We heard lots of stories that it was in fact an IRA pub, and we were warned by our parents and neighbours to stay well away from it. Our front room overlooked the pub's backyard. I used to spend hours watching the comings and goings of – to me – a number of shady characters. I did earn a couple of pounds when asked by the landlord to move some furniture from the pub into a removal van. When inside the pub, I was disappointed not to see any terrorist paraphernalia, AK47s or hand grenades – I did have quite an imagination. They were probably in the beer cellar. However, they did have the biggest German shepherd dog I had ever seen.

On the other side of Burnt Oak Broadway was the grand Odeon cinema where Ray and I would go on Saturday mornings with our sixpence pocket money. We would firstly visit the pick and mix in Woolworths next door to the cinema and spend half the money and then use the other half to get into the cinema. There would always be a cartoon followed by a main feature film. The Odeon was a huge cinema with a capacity of 1,476 seats. It was eventually closed in 1972 and demolished a few years later.

My parents still struggled to pay the rent. I vividly remember taking my brother Ray, who is three years younger than me, into the bedroom to hide – we thought it was a game, especially when all the lights went out. It was due to the rent man working his way down the street. Mum used to join us, and we all giggled as he rapped on the front door several times before giving up. Of course, it meant paying two weeks' rent the next time he called. The kitchen and bathroom were tiny and in bad condition, in fact, downright dangerous. Mum found out the hard way. Whilst having a bath, she received an electric shock from one of the taps. An electrician had to rewire the whole premises. I was too ashamed to bring any school friends back home due to its dilapidated appearance.

The old place finally gave up the ghost when I was twelve. Dad was now a coach driver and often away from home on long-haul coach trips to the Continent for two or three weeks at a time. One of his proudest memories as a coach driver was driving the West Indies cricket team around the UK on one of their UK tours.

In the early seventies, Dad was taking a party to a European beer festival and, for the first time, took Mum with him; I think it was the only occasion she ever left these shores. It was a short trip over a long weekend. Mum wouldn't have left Ray and my youngest brother Shaun, who was two or three years of age, and I, for any longer. My maternal grandmother travelled over from Wembley to look after us; they had moved from Vine Court in Kenton to Kings Drive, a short distance from the then Brent Town Hall. On the Saturday night, there was a terrific storm which brought the ceiling of the small kitchen of 12A down and flooded the first floor of the maisonette. Nan packed us all up and took us home to Wembley. Within a few days, the council condemned 12A and offered us a three-bedroomed house in a quiet residential road: Rushden Gardens in Mill Hill. I still remember Mum's face as she walked into No. 11. It was a standard terraced council house, but she said it was like Buckingham Palace.

For the first time, aged thirteen, I had my own bedroom: a small box room at the front of the house. I had started at Edgware secondary school two years earlier, and Ray was just about to start there as well. It was a fair journey from Mill Hill: two buses and a short walk. Dad had left coaching and was now a bus driver for London Transport based at Hendon bus garage, which meant we saw a lot more of him than when he was coaching. Mill Hill was a nice place to live: plenty of open spaces and good transport links both bus and underground; Mill Hill East station was a ten-minute walk.

A short walk from the house was Hendon Golf Club. On a Saturday morning, Ray and I would stand outside the clubhouse, often in the pouring rain, and wait for the golfers to come out and start their rounds. Many of them couldn't be bothered to pull or carry their golf clubs around the course, so they would hire one of us boys as a caddy. Golfers, I found, could be a rather intolerant bunch. It was quite amusing to watch some of them, dressed like Nick Faldo, with top-of-the-range equipment, put their first ball into the trees – of course they would blame the wind or the rain, even the poor thirteen-year-old caddy, hence my lifetime hatred of the game of golf.

Blame the Caddy

I've never had the golfing bug,
In fact, I'd prefer to wrap myself in a flea-infested rug.
Pringle jumpers and tasselled shoes,
A few of hours walking before hitting the booze.

The latest clubs or irons you must be seen to own,
Playing with a cheaper ball your partner cannot condone.
If you slice a shot and throw a little paddy,
You just hunch your shoulders and blame the poor old caddy.

Another wayward shot demands a call of fore!
It hits a fellow golfer who now lays comatose on the floor.
The iron slipped, you explain to your fellow golfer, who's bleeding rather badly,
You huff and puff and blame the poor old caddy.

Eighteenth hole now completed,
You return to the clubhouse soundly defeated.
Not accepting for a minute that you played at all badly,
You just turn around, with a contemptuous smile, and blame the poor old caddy.

In the early 1980s, Mum, aged in her fifties, passed her driving test and became much more independent. She began working at the Inglis British Army Barracks and postal depot in Mill Hill East, as a secretary to the housing commandant. The barracks were occupied by the Royal Engineers at the time. The late 1970s, in particular, had seen a sustained campaign of terror by the Provisional Irish Republican Army (PIRA). This campaign continued throughout the 1980s and 1990s. She had a lucky escape on the 1st of August 1988 when PIRA planted a bomb on the complex which exploded without warning at 7am, killing one soldier and injuring nine others. Mum had been due to start work at 8am. It didn't faze her – she was back at her desk as soon as the barracks were reopened.

Neither my two brothers nor I were destined for university. Firstly, our parents couldn't have afforded to send us, and secondly, all three of us hated school and finished with negligible qualifications. I managed a couple of CSEs and one O level in religious education – I was never destined for the church, even though, up to the age of twelve or thirteen, we were kicked out of the house by Mum every Sunday morning to attend Sunday school, whilst still living in Burnt Oak. It was her rest time over the weekend.

As soon as I could (fifteen years and ten months), I left school and got a casual job in the Macfisheries supermarket in Station Road, Edgware next to Edgware underground station. I initially applied to join the Royal Navy, but they couldn't, or wouldn't, offer the career opportunities I wanted – probably due to my lack of qualifications. I could have gone in as an able seaman but chose not to – the only regret I have in life. I decided that I would wait until I was eighteen and apply to the police force.
I was already well into my darts. I loved the game and had an opportunity to play for a pub team in Hendon called The

Chequers. I had only just turned seventeen when I played my first game for the pub. We travelled all over north-west London playing in the Queensbury darts league. The high point was competing in the *Daily Mirror* junior darts championships. It was the day after my eighteenth birthday and took place at the Michael Sobell sports centre in Holloway. I lost in the North London final. But I did meet my darting heroes of the time: Eric Bristow and Alan Glazier, who presented me with a set of dart flights (which he probably dished out to everybody else) that I still have to this day, along with my runners-up medal. My darts career would come to an abrupt end when I did join the police and started to work shifts.

Aged sixteen, I started to get an interest in weight training. I trained with Hendon bus garage's tug of war team which I soon became a member of. I've never really been a team sports player, but tug of war is a fantastic team sport and I loved it. The training was extremely hard, especially as the other members were all in their twenties and thirties and much stronger, but I held my own. We would train in a sports field in Kingsbury. The main focus of a training session would be pulling an oil drum, filled with concrete, affixed to a scaffold, up and down, holding it for minutes at a time at its highest and lowest levels. We entered several competitions, including the Middlesex championships, and gave our all. We were never particularly successful, as there were many semi-professional teams around the county and country. It was the first time I really felt part of something. I'm not a fan of clichés, but I did turn from a boy into a man.

Tug of War

Eight versus eight – it's quite a thrill,
No tougher test of human strength and zeal.
A rope just short of thirty-four metres long,
Pulled with hands that grip tight and strong.

Competitions normally take place on grass,
And are contested in weights of a differing class.
One such pull across a stream,
Ended with wet feet for the losing team.

Four metres is the distance each team aims to pull,
Hobnail boots embedded deep to prevent a fall.
The flag goes down; muscles tense;
The pulling force is truly immense.

The stronger team gets into their stride,
The weaker falters, slips and slides.
Reacting to the coach's call,
The victorious team shouts and bawls.

One last effort to cross the line,
One final heave, all in time.
The other team realises the game is up,
The winners get a cheer and a silver cup.

Just after my seventeenth birthday, I was promoted to Fruit and Vegetable Manager at Macfisheries in North Finchley. It was a small department in quite a large supermarket, and I found myself lumbered with a member of staff – my only one apart from a Saturday casual – who was probably the laziest individual I've ever come across. He was a little peeved that I, his manager, was several years younger than he was; that was his problem. I put up with it for several weeks until I had my feet under the table and then I transferred him to another department. I realised at that moment I wasn't supervisor material, which goes some way to explaining why I never strived for any higher rank in the police force.

Once I had turned eighteen (the earliest age you could apply), I put my application in for two police forces – the Metropolitan Police and the British Transport Police (BTP). I had an interview and entrance exam at the BTP recruitment centre in Paddington in late September 1977. I remember reading a highlighted article from *The Times* newspaper and taking a simple arithmetic test before being informed that – subject to some vetting – I was in. I soon received a starting date. I submitted my resignation to the general manager at Macfisheries with a heavy heart. I loved my time working for the company and have always been grateful for the opportunities they had given me. I felt even worse when the general manager Mr Les Chennels – whom I had the greatest respect for – thought my letter was a Christmas card. Sadly, within a year, Macfisheries had disappeared from the British high street, taken over by another retailer.

I started my new career, which would last for thirty-three years, on the 6th of February 1978, three weeks after turning eighteen and a half. I immediately hit some highs and lows. The high was the publication of the *Edmund Davies Report* into police pay and conditions. The report recommended a substantial rise in police pay which I received almost immediately in my wage packet; I was now earning more than double the amount I was at Macfisheries. The lows: firstly, being informed that I was too young to go out on the beat and would have to wait until I was nineteen; secondly, being told by a crusty old police constable, who had proudly fought in the Second World War with the medal ribbons to show for it, that 'the job was f****d'.

On my nineteenth birthday in July 1978, I was finally let out on the loose. Every police officer holds a view that *their* time was the best – a little like the war hero – and I am no different – I loved the job. A police force was run on the basis of discipline and a respect for the chain of command – sadly, it has changed.

The Thin Blue Line

I joined the police force in the '70s, when only eighteen,
I wasn't exactly *Dixon of Dock Green*.
Before every duty we would stand on parade,
We were given our tasks which were unquestioningly obeyed.

Our truncheons and whistles were produced for inspection,
Our pocket books examined for mistakes and corrections.
We were a band of brothers and sisters – a thin line of blue,
Who would protect each other's backs against the criminal few.

We took an oath to serve and protect,
Discipline coupled with pride and respect.
Always a brave face against the fist and the knife,
Through the stress and the strife, this was a job for life.

With the closure of many police stations, the bobby now a rare sight,
Today we seem to be losing the criminal fight.
Senior officers with *woke* agendas and a lack of backbone,
Leave some fine men and women to fight on their own.

Shoplifters steal whatever and whenever they like,
We watch as our crime figures annually spike.
Kids roam in gangs, armed with knife,
Belligerent, caring little for the sanctity of life.

Now we have chief constables with *brand-new* ideas,
Police officers on street corners will allay people's fears.
Thank God these chief officers all have degrees,
Just sounds like good old common sense to me.

I hope they sort out this policing mess,
And alleviate front-line officers' levels of stress.
They are, God bless them, in the main, dedicated to the cause,
To arrest wrongdoers and uphold our democratic laws.

Most police officers will experience, early on in their careers, a defining moment when they confirm to themselves, beyond doubt, this is the job for them or not. My defining moment came very quickly at the Notting Hill Carnival in 1978. We had been deployed to Ladbroke Grove tube station on the Hammersmith and City line right in the middle of the carnival area. The carnival takes place over the August bank holiday weekend. The Sunday is generally known as 'children's day' and normally passes peacefully. The Monday has a different vibe about it. The happy, smiling faces of children and their parents are replaced with hostility and aggression from gangs who travel from all over London to steal and rob. The event in the previous two years had ended in extreme violence against the police, who were ill-prepared in relation to equipment and public order tactics; things hadn't changed much by August of 1978.

A Hot Summer's Night (1978)

A young man in uniform,
Buttons gleaming,
Whistles blowing,
Children screaming.

A serial of cops stand in wait,
Violence in the air they anticipate.
Colourful floats and dancers soon disappear,
Replaced by feelings of anxiety and fear.

Cars ablaze, the howl of the crowd,
Feelings of hatred cast aloud.
Bricks, bins and bottles fly through the air,
Aimed at a line of blue looking back in despair.

Rioters advance with criminal intent,
Full of anger they feel they must vent.
The exhilaration of Carnival doesn't last,
The streets are buried under broken glass.

A Hammersmith and City line train runs through the scene,
Electric sparks bright under wheels that scream.
An avalanche of missiles breaks the carriage glass,
Passengers cowering, hoping to pass.

This area of West London, home to the rich and the poor,
Where black and white communities live door to door,
Brush themselves down and get on with their lives,
Notting Hill returns to its passive vibe.

From that moment on, I knew this was the job for me. The fear and the adrenaline rush were addictive. Every day and night was different, exciting – a new experience every single time I came on duty, never knowing what I was going to face. The camaraderie and banter was infectious. Then I went to my first person under a train – colloquially referred to as a 'One Under'. In the 1970s and 1980s, it was a frequent event – committing suicide by jumping under a train on both the main line and London Underground rail systems. With improved platform and track design, it is not such a frequent event nowadays, but people still end, or attempt to end (death is certainly not guaranteed), their lives by this method. I attended my first incident of this nature in 1979. It was an event that delivered a harsh reality. Not due to the nature of the injuries – they were barely visible – but more the realisation that such a young girl, with her whole life in front of her, had been so desperate she could see no other way out but to end her life in this tragic way. On the day of the incident, I spoke to the tube train driver involved, a devout Muslim, who gave me his account of what had happened. The train drivers are often the forgotten victim in these incidents; many suffer mental distress years after. In remembrance of the young girl who died at the scene, even though it is almost a half a century ago, I have changed her name and omitted the location.

What a Waste

What could I do? She was standing right there.
Air from the tunnel blowing her hair,
She looked at me with a deathly stare,
Though her life was over she didn't care.

My instincts kicked in as she fell down below,
Time stood still as I screamed at her – No!
I looked away as I heard the brakes hiss,
I prayed to my God that it'd been a near miss.

Now on the platform I shouted under the train,
Desperate for her to answer and absolve me from blame.
My anger at her for what she had done,
Disappeared when I thought of *my* young son.

The police arrived, paramedics too,
I felt really sick and needed the loo.
Twenty-seven years driving an underground train,
Never had I felt so much sorrow and pain.

As the train moved forward, I knew she was dead,
But I couldn't avert my eyes and looked down with dread.
She was blonde and beautiful, not a scratch could be seen,
A police officer told me her name was Kathleen.

I gave evidence to a court of law,
Explaining to a jury what I saw.
I was informed that Kathleen was a mother and a wife,
Oh, what a waste of such a young life.

Having been born in North West London, and having had an uncle who was an Arsenal fanatic, I had little choice of which side of North London I would support: the Reds. My first game at Highbury when I was seven years old, in the company of Uncle Alby, is one of few childhood memories I still hold. The floodlights, the smell of the food and the noise of the crowd growing louder as you approached the ground.

As a uniformed police officer, I was regularly posted to a football match on a Saturday. Obviously, being a member of the Transport Police, we policed the London Underground on which most supporters, both home and away, would travel to get to the matches. The 1970s and '80s were notorious for football violence both in the grounds and on the transport system. The tube system, at times, was like a battleground – I loved it. In general, the football gangs were cowards: often happy to be part of a large gang but, when opposed by police officers in much smaller numbers, would usually run.

A location where there was always violence on a Saturday afternoon was the temporary coach station on the site of an old railway goods yard on Euston Road between St Pancras and Euston stations. This was an era before football was played on a Sunday or Monday at differing kick-off times. Every game started at 3pm on a Saturday afternoon. The coach station, which had a capacity for many dozens of coaches, was situated on land that the British Library was built on and which opened in 1997. You can imagine the chaos and potential for violence when rival supporters arrived back at the coach station all at the same time on match days. The Euston Road was frequently a battleground: the fighting football thugs versus police.

Being an avid Arsenal fan, I was always pleased to be posted to Arsenal or Finsbury Park stations. When the forward traffic had moved through to the ground, we would be stood down for our meal. If you chose to, you could go and watch the game. We used to go onto the upper tier of the West Stand. The only downside was dealing with anything that happened in the ground whilst we were there, which was quite unusual in that particular stand, but also having to leave and be back on post fifteen minutes before the final whistle.

The Football Match

The home fans arrive at Arsenal station,
Mingling with opposing supporters from around the nation.
The excitement grows in anticipation,
Of the impending sporting confrontation.

Out the tube and onto the streets,
Taking in the aroma from the foody treats.
As kick-off nears, the crowd gravitates,
Towards the floodlights and entrance gates.

Supporters veer around some bothersome touts,
'Get your programmes here,' the seller shouts.
The roar of the crowd, the filling of the ground,
Policemen keeping a watchful eye all around.

Kick-off time is nearly here,
The players run out to a massive cheer.
The home team are waving, dressed in red and white,
The noise of the crowd reaches a deafening height.

The North Bank sings its normal songs,
Encouraging the Clock End to respond.
A small section of the opposing fans,
Raise and gesticulate with their hands.

The whistle is blown at the end of the half,
Another forty-five minutes of this is no laugh.
Those who are about to burst,
Have to decide what comes first,
A dash to the toilets for a lash,

Or back to the bar and splash the cash.

The second half is just as dire,
The Gunners' cannon fails to fire.
A nil-nil draw is the result,
The crowd leaves in silence as if in a sulk.

The journey home on public transport will be long,
No more banter to be heard, nor a cheery song.
Get those spirits up in time to start another working day,
The next home game's only two weeks away.

I passed through my probationary period of two years; my enthusiasm for the job I was doing never wavered. But I did start to think of the future – did I want to stay in uniform and maybe pass my promotion exams? As I've stated before, I was no scholar, but I did have a serious attempt at the sergeant's exam and failed by a few marks. That was a mixed blessing in relation to my later years of service. In the period between Christmas and New Year 1981/2, I was given an opportunity that would change the direction of my career. I was offered an attachment to the Pickpocket Squad that operated on the London Underground. I never wore a police uniform again.

The Thieves

Two thieves skulk in a passageway,
Watching, waiting, for their prey.
Busy commuters passing by,
Observed intently by an expert eye.

Victim identified, they wait for the rattle,
And watch, amused, as passengers engage in battle.
The thieves move apart, victim in sight,
She is unaware of her impending plight.

The train screams in with headlights glaring,
The crush of people – tempers flaring.
The two thieves move in for the kill,
Removing her purse with agility and skill.

They back off slowly, their mission complete,
Freeing themselves, light on their feet.
So eager to examine their ill-gotten gains,
Awareness around them they fail to maintain.

When strong hands grab and twist their collars,
They fight and kick, scream and holler.
The thieves to the ground, they are felled,
The violence they offer quickly quelled.

They plead their innocence to passers-by;
Handcuffs are aggressively applied.
The victim comes forward and is reunited with her purse;
The thieves in the distance swear and curse.

The Pickpocket Squad was a great policing education. It would be another couple of years before the implementation of the Crown Prosecution Service. Police officers were still taking cases to the magistrates' court, dealing with bail applications and committal proceedings. Sadly, nowadays, police officers rarely attend court until the trial stage – many may not gain the experience of giving evidence until much later in their careers.

After eighteen months trailing around the London Underground looking for pickpockets, I became a detective constable in 1983. I completed my CID course in Preston, Lancashire and was stationed at Baker Street in the divisional CID office.

Late 1983, I decided it was time to move; home was getting a little crowded and – at times, as you would expect with three brothers – a little tense. I'd saved hard, working all the overtime I could get, and put together a reasonable-sized deposit for a ground-floor maisonette in Windsor Road, High Barnet; if I remember correctly, I purchased it for £25,000.

In early 1984, Baker Street CID moved into some temporary accommodation at 116 Baker Street due to some renovation work being carried out on a new police station called Selbie House. It was a beautiful sunny day in April 1984 when I left 116 Baker Street to go on an inquiry, when my life changed forever.

116 Baker Street

I met her first in Baker Street,
She was young, smart and light on her feet.
She smiled at me with eyes so blue,
What came over me – I hadn't a clue.
She was so beautiful, I so plain,
I never thought I'd see her again.

I admired her with a secret glance,
Until one night I took my chance.
We met in a crowded Baker Street pub,
Tongue-tied, I expected a snub.

Within three months we were engaged,
In December of that same year we would marry,
The first of our three children she would soon carry.

Thirty plus years we have reached,
Our feelings for each other have never been breached.
Some highs and some lows along the way,
But by her side I will ever stay.
A frightening year has just gone past,
But we share a love that will always last.

In August 1985, our first child, Gavin, arrived. I was working at the Notting Hill Carnival and arrived home just as Karen was being taken to the maternity ward at Barking Hospital in East London; she gave birth in the early hours of the morning. I was due to give evidence at Southwark Crown Court the following morning but, luckily, a sympathetic judge was prepared to delay my evidence to the following day.

By this time, we had moved to a three-bedroomed terraced house in Balfour Road, Ilford. A couple of months before Gavin arrived, I had to sell my beloved MKV Cortina to enable us to install central heating. We lived in Balfour Road for the next ten years or so and had our two daughters – Hayley and Nicola – in 1987 and 1989 respectively. I had two brothers and a son; Karen had a brother, Peter, so I was pretty shocked to be handed two beautiful daughters. I'm very proud of my three children, who have grown up and found their way in the world. Yes, of course, as with any family, there have been a few hiccups on the way, but they have adopted our family trait of getting their heads down and working hard.

Professionally, I moved around quite a bit, spending no more than four years in the same place. These included spells at Stockwell CID, Clapham and Putney police stations on murder inquiries and then to BTP's surveillance team at the former headquarters in Tavistock Place WC1 in 1993.

This was a testing time for the family as I was required to work away from home on a regular basis. It reminded me of my own childhood with my father travelling away regularly and how my mum coped with us three boys. Karen was incredible during this time, somehow managing to look after the three children and hold down several jobs of her own. Money was tight, so the overtime I earned and Karen's jobs got us through. It would often work out that I would be away in the week and home at the weekends when she would go out to work. Our parents helped out greatly during this time. Shortly after we moved into Balfour Road, we bought a dog: Bruno, a Boxer. He was my escape route whenever I needed to clear my head. We would walk miles. He was my dog.

In 1997, we moved from Ilford a mile up the road to Martley Drive, Gants Hill to enable all three of our children to have a bedroom of their own. Within a year, Bruno became quite ill and had to be put down.

My Loyal Friend

With a flattish face that always looked sad,
He was the most loyal friend I've ever had.
I could chat and moan on our long daily walks,
He'd just trot alongside me and never talk.

He was seven stone of muscle and bone,
As strong as an ox. As sly as a fox.
He could be as stubborn as a mule,
But he was nobody's fool.

Fiercely protective of my children and wife,
I was in no doubt he would've protected them with his life.
He was no lover of garden flowers,
And would often cover us in a spittle shower.

He was never too keen on other dogs,
When approached by one, he would go to ground,
Before attacking them from below,
Defeated, off they would bound.

We would go to the forest or park at night,
Where he could run freely, well out of sight.
He liked to play his fun and games,
Hitting me full on with all his might.

I trained him well,
He would walk to heel.
When approaching a road, he would automatically sit,
He would even pull me to the kerb so he could have a… poo.

He lasted for a whole decade,
A family legend, full of escapades.
The trip to the vets to end his life,
Cut through me like a razor-sharp knife.

He looked at me with those big soulful eyes,
With his last breath, I swear he said goodbye.
I loved that dog with all my heart,
Thank you, my loyal friend – death do us part.

We settled into our new house which had been renovated by a builder – a jack of all trades and master of none. Within the first couple of days, we discovered that the washing machine outlet was blocked which flooded the kitchen; the fuse box was a fire hazard; and the boiler was on its last legs. The kids went to nearby schools and Gants Hill station on the London Underground's Central line was a short walk away. When you are a Londoner, you tend to take the tube for granted. Yes, it could be infuriating when not working properly, but it gave access to anywhere in the capital all within an hour.

A Journey on the Central Line

How we moan, whinge and whine,
About our dear old Central line.
Leaves on the track, signals at fault,
Conspire to bring our trains to a halt.

A blood-red vein passing through the heart of our city,
Along lines and tracks of immense complexity.
From Epping in the east to Ealing in the west,
A service that can put our patience to the test.

Passengers travel in a robotic style,
Never exchanging a friendly smile.
Jostling and pushing with elbows and knees,
Frayed tempers produce a feeling of unease.

Crammed into the carriage like sardines in a can,
Sweaty armpits,
A pungent scent,
An ideal place for a thief with intent.

A greasy head rests against a glass divide,
In a timely motion it glides from side to side,
Eyes firmly shut, pretending to sleep.
'Baby on board' states a badge on a chest,
Our sleeper takes a sly little peep,
An expression translates a hopeful plea,
But eyes stay shut, ignoring the mother-to-be.

Oxford Circus, Marble Arch, Tottenham Court Road,
Shoppers board with their heavy loads.
Packages and presents at Xmas time,
Children excited, desperate to tweet,
Exhausted parents dead on their feet.

We love our Central line now open all night,
Some brand-new stations gleaming and bright.
As we tap in and out and descend below ground,
Listening for that familiar sound,
A train rattling in, slowing to a stop,
Doors open and on we gratefully hop.

All stations to Hainault via Newbury Park,
Party-goers excited, having a lark.
I snuggle down, feeling pretty fine,
Where would I be without my Central line?

I spent four years at BTP headquarters and loved the work. As a national police force, the team worked all over the United Kingdom, dealing with a variety of serious offences from theft of the Royal Mail to drugs and armed robbery. After a couple of years, I would train other members of the force in surveillance techniques. This was the first time I had ever presented in front of a class, and I enjoyed it. It would be something that I developed over the coming years and gave me the confidence to become a public speaker, which I still do today.

In 1995, I started to develop an interest in writing. I had always been fascinated by London's history and had an idea about writing a book on the subject one day. I did some research and discovered that a definitive history of the London Square hadn't been written since 1910. I started to do some research into the subject, but that's as far as it went as, unbeknown to me, a huge challenge was just around the corner.

In 1997, I was given the opportunity to be posted to the Anti-Terrorist Branch (SO13) based on the fifteenth floor of New Scotland Yard, at the time on Broadway, St James's Park. It was a huge opportunity, and I discussed it with Karen, who was very supportive even though it would mean long hours and again being away from home at very short notice. Financially, it was a very good move; the family were growing and so were the costs to support them. I started in January of that year.

The threat from the Provisional Irish Republican Army (PIRA) had soon diminished with the signing of the Good Friday Agreement. But, almost immediately, we were faced with a threat from dissident groups who were not on board with the treaty. It was also a time when we saw the emergence of al Qaeda and other Islamic extremist groups, firstly around the world and then on home soil. The first bomb scene I attended was in

Brixton in April 1999. When we were expecting attacks from Irish dissident groups, Islamic fundamentalists and even animal rights groups, nobody really saw this coming.

The Brixton Bomb

It is beyond most people's comprehension,
That a bomb could be placed with such evil intention.
To kill and maim innocent passers-by,
Just makes one want to scream and cry.

A thriving Brixton Market with vendors selling all their wares,
A happy family atmosphere, no one with any cares.
As the sun began to set, life would change very fast,
They looked around, confused and scared, totally aghast.

A bomb scattering its shrapnel, flying red hot through the air,
Ripped through human skin and bone as if it wasn't there.
Children, women, the elderly, it didn't discriminate,
The bomber had left his deadly package, and the innocent, to their fate.

Sadly, he would attack again; deliver his deadly load,
Was it a race war he was desperately trying to goad?
Two further attacks – four people dead,
Fear among Londoners quickly spread.

This white supremacist murderer was relentlessly hunted down,
And promptly brought before the courts and prosecuted by the Crown.
His hatred for his victims was chillingly so real,
The only human emotion, apparently, he could feel.

A full life sentence means he'll never see the light of day,
Incarcerated in Broadmoor where he will surely stay.
All we can do in remembrance to those injured and who died is state,
There is no tolerance in this country for such evil, pernicious hate.

I remained at New Scotland Yard for seven and a half years. At times it was hard, particularly on my family. I remember calling Karen when she was at work to tell her I was just about to fly out to Athens in Greece. I couldn't tell her why or when I would be back. Probably the most testing occurrence was a few days after the World Trade Center attack in New York in September 2001. I had recently qualified in the role of a family liaison officer; some colleagues and I were deployed to New York to support the families of those British subjects who were believed to have lost their lives. We were to take the first flight allowed from Britain to New York since the attack. Karen was extremely worried and didn't want me to go – it was a very stressful time. In the end, we were in New York for just over two weeks.

New York was a little like London. It was back on its feet within days. The site itself was mind-blowing; the pictures beamed around the world of the remains of the World Trade Center and surrounding buildings never did justice to the horror and destruction. I dealt with several families who travelled over to New York in the hope that their relative may be found. There were many stories circulating in the media about people escaping certain death by being late for work or having a dental appointment or reporting in sick. Many of these people went off the radar for days, unable to cope with the fact that they had lost their work colleagues, their jobs and feeling guilty that they had survived. This did give every relative hope that their loved one may be wandering around New York dazed and traumatised by these events and could still be found alive. Sadly, this was never the case.

The American law enforcement agencies implemented a remarkable forensic recovery operation. Millions of fragments of human bone and tissue were recovered from the scene over months and years, identified by DNA and returned, where possible, to the families. One family I looked after whilst in New York received a piece of thigh bone back, after several months of living hell, which allowed them to hold a funeral and helped them to come to terms with their loss.

The twin towers attack had a profound effect on Americans. This was the first time in their history they had been struck by terrorists, on home soil, on such a major scale. Americans had now experienced the devastation of terrorism on their own doorstep.

The next four years were a blur: dozens of investigations and travel around the world and within the United Kingdom. I finally moved back to the BTP in August 2004. In the meantime, Karen had put herself through City University, and qualified as a speech and language therapist. I was a very proud husband when she graduated in the ornate surroundings of the Guildhall, London. Gavin had left school and joined the Royal Navy, and the two girls were young adults. I did return to SO13 in 2005 as part of the investigation team into the 7th of July London bombings on the tube and Tavistock Square.

I was now acutely aware that I had twenty-seven years of service, although I would have to serve thirty-one and a half years before I could retire at the age of fifty. On returning to BTP, I was back on divisional CID, which I found difficult to adjust to. So much had changed in the eight years or so I had been away. The downside to being on such a specialised squad as SO13 was you became de-skilled in other general policing areas, especially around new computer systems that had been introduced.

I was rescued from the conundrum I faced, where I seriously considered leaving the police and finding another path in life, by a training opportunity that came out of the 7/7 bombings. The force adopted a behavioural detection training course introduced by the United States after the 9/11 attacks. A colleague of mine, whom I had served with at FHQ – Mick London – and I were the two main trainers to roll out the programme nationally for the next four to five years.

My mind returned to writing the London Square book. I started to use some of my spare time that I was now enjoying to begin writing in earnest.

Squares of London

Anybody with time to spare,
Must visit one of London's squares.
Square, rectangular, straight or round,
History, architecture, blue plaques abound.

The first, Covent Garden, rose from the slums,
Commissioned by a local lord for a tidy sum.
Inigo Jones, inspired by visits to Rome,
Designed and built it on his return home.

Bloomsbury and St James's would soon follow,
In Dorset Square you could hear leather on willow.
Thomas Lord sold up as quickly as he could,
Now the famous ground's home is in St John's Wood.

Landscaped gardens under lock and key,
Are enjoyed by residents for a fee.
Trees and shrubs, fragrant flowers,
Bring pleasure and solace hour after hour.

Tavistock Square promotes tranquillity and peace,
An oasis amongst London's concrete beasts.
A space in which author Virginia Woolf would roam,
Where she could work and rest so close to home.

Central Square in Golders Green,
Two finer Lutyens churches cannot be seen,
One domed, one steepled, they rise to the sky,
Almost touching the clouds floating high and by.

So as you twist and turn through London's streets,
Give yourself a rare old treat,
Step into and discover one of its historic squares,
And uncover the raft of history that will be lying there.

The Four Corners of St James's Square

In a quiet corner of St James's Square,
Can be found a reader's lair.
A building of insignificance to a passer-by,
Contains a million books stacked floor to sky.
A place where Carlyle and Dickens trained their minds,
Is truly, truly, a wonderful find.

A rain of bullets fired from the people's bureau,
By some unknown Libyan 'hero'.
Parted a protesting crowd,
Who ducked, dived and screamed aloud.

As the dust came to settle and to rest,
A young police constable lay upon the ground,
With her colleagues all around,
Their efforts were sadly in vain,
As her life's blood began to slowly drain.
A nearby stone reminds us that our memories should never fade,
Of the sacrifice young Yvonne Fletcher made.

Norfolk House on the south-east corner,
Was the headquarters of an influential soldier.
From within this building Eisenhower took the course,
Of directing the European and US Allied force.

The decisions took within these walls,
Ultimately lead to the Nazi fall.

Four corners of course make up a square,
So we cannot possibly finish there.

In the south-west corner made of glass,
Is a building which underlines true English class.
Drinks and stories abound as old shoulders rub,
In the Army and Navy gentlemen's club.

The London Plane

The London Plane tree with its mottled bark,
Is an impressive sight in light or dark.
It breathes in all the city grime,
And spits it out at harvest time.

A familiar feature of squares and parks,
A nightingale can be heard if one harks.
Lovers cuddle; the homeless sleep,
Under its great branches twenty or so deep.

Dozens of Plane trees – some hundreds of years old –
Defy London's weather be it hot or cold.
When it sheds its pollen during a late spring breeze,
It can, unfortunately, make us sneeze.

But in these days of climate change,
When floods and fire are in our range,
We must protect our trees with all our might,
So our children's children can share in their delight.

The Monument

On Fish Street Hill – junction with Monument Street –
Rises a Doric column two hundred and two feet.
Three hundred and twelve steps to the top it's true,
But the effort is worth it for WOW what a view.

A monument built by Wren and by Hook,
To commemorate a great fire recorded in history books.
A fire that raged four days and four nights,
Burning buildings and churches alight.
Londoners were truly transfixed,
In the year of Our Lord sixteen sixty-six.

'A woman could piss it out,' ingenuously the Lord Mayor of London cried,
Miraculously only three people died.
Conspiracy theories circulated about,
'The Catholics are guilty,' many cried,
Forcing innocent citizens to run and hide.

If you pass this pillar of Portland stone,
On any map it will be shown,
Spend a few pennies and enjoy the view,
As you may be among the very last few,
As towers of metal and of glass,
Push our capital's history firmly to the past.

When Karen and I got married in December 1984, we delayed our honeymoon until January 1985 so we could go to Italy skiing. We travelled to just north of Milan to spend two weeks in a ski resort in the picturesque town of Aprica. However, days before we travelled, Karen discovered that she was pregnant so wasn't allowed to ski or ice skate, so although we were delighted with the news, morning sickness dictated the tone of the holiday, and we were just glad to get back home.

Of course, from then onwards, family and financial constraints took over. I travelled extensively throughout my career, both nationally and internationally, and developed a great dislike for airports. Although we did try to return to Italy, we, as a couple, were destined never to travel abroad again.

The Ash Cloud

Spring 2010 we were Roma bound,
But our flight was cancelled, and we remained on the ground.
An Icelandic volcano had lost its cool,
We all laughed, thinking it was an April Fool.

It spewed its toxic plume miles up towards space,
Hiding the sun without a trace.
As the grey dust wafted south and west,
Europe could only wait and hope for the best.

Plans abandoned, our Euros exchanged,
Nothing else prearranged.
Passports replaced, luggage stowed,
We jumped into the car and hit the road.

We travelled from our B and B,
With the intention of heading towards the sea.
A quick turn to the west,
And we settled on Salisbury as second best.

A nice weekend was had by all,
A lovely city, a tall steeple.
We headed back towards our home,
Rueing the trip we'd missed to Rome.

Researching for *Square London: A Social History of the Iconic London Square* (the title I had chosen for the book) was extensive. I hadn't realised how big a task I was embarking on. The first task was counting how many squares there were in London. It amounted to nine hundred, give or take. I stumbled on a defining parameter for the book by accident. I visited a square in Marylebone, having researched it online and then through more reliable sources (as I did with all the squares in the book), to find that only a small passageway, bearing the square's name, remained. I was pretty disappointed and didn't want somebody reading my book to go out and explore and have the same unsatisfactory experience. So, from then on, the square had to exist in much of its original form for it to be included. I eventually narrowed it down to 114. I spent hours and hours in the squares I was researching and in bookshops, libraries and stationers all over London.

The Bookshop

A place for contemplation with a murmur of chat,
Not quite a library but something akin to that.
You discover works by authors you have often favoured,
In a place where you won't be subject to antisocial behaviour.

Row upon row, shelf upon shelf,
Thousands of books in which to delve.
From crime fiction to poetry, history to romance,
Geographical works on Germany and France.

Knowledgeable staff can help with advice and direction,
To biographies and the children's section.
Comfy chairs are available if you look,
In which you can sink and relax with a book.

Those not interested in books can still meet and greet,
With many bookshops offering coffee and sweet treats.
The humble bookshop, be it independent or a chain,
Provides us with a sanctuary and shelter from the rain.

I'm a Papyrophiliac

I have an obsession that I must divulge,
An old-age habit in which I indulge.
I cannot pass a stationary store,
Without stepping in to browse and explore.

The aroma of paper and printing ink,
The multicoloured Post-its in orange, yellow and pink.
From self-assembly desks to tiny pins and paperclips,
Blotting paper, address books and charts that flip.

The superstores stacked from ceiling to floor,
A papyrophiliac I am for evermore.
In our times of smartphones, tablets and Excel sheets,
With the opening of a virgin notebook, they cannot hope to compete.

Luxury designs with a tactile feel,
Sturdy binders with rings of steel.
Assorted key rings and plastic fobs,
Endless stickers and bits and bobs.

Personalised gifts with gold or silver initials,
Party invitations with balloons and whistles.
A fountain pen from which real ink flows,
And which one can create imaginary prose.

As I walk from aisle to aisle,
Each corner I turn broadens my smile,
I can lose myself for hours in this stationary wonder,
A space I'll enjoy until I'm six feet under.

I completed my thirty years' police service in February 2008 but had at least another eighteen months before I was eligible for retirement aged fifty. The research for *Square London* was going well, and I had started to draft the chapters and take some photographs for inclusion. In 2009, another opportunity appeared with retirement in mind from a source that I'd never considered. Sitting on the tube on the way into work, I was reading *The Metro*, a free London newspaper. I glanced down to the very bottom of the vacancies page to spot a tiny three- or four-lined advert for volunteers to work in St Paul's Cathedral. I applied and was successful. Due to still working Monday to Friday, and the occasional weekend, as a police training officer, I opted to work one Sunday a month. I hadn't been in St Paul's Cathedral since I was a child (in truth I can't even remember that visit). I walked in to meet my new team on Remembrance Sunday, November 2009. I was in absolute awe at the magnificence of the building. Jumping ahead a little, in 2013 I enrolled on the cathedral guiding course and passed out as a qualified guide in April 2014. I joined the brilliant Wednesday team and, to this day, am still guiding people around this wonderful building.

A Nation's Cathedral

Wren's St Paul's stands proudly Baroque,
As Tom bellows out from Grimthorpe's clock.
Tourists chatter; Christians pray,
Under the high dome three hundred feet away.

Vestments in green, purple or white,
Glitter and sparkle in candlelight.
Blake Richmond's mosaics reflect a setting sun,
As the choir sings, without a glitch,
Evensong sung at perfect pitch.

England's naval hero immortalised in stone,
A lion foreboding, guarding alone.
At Trafalgar he faced Napoleon's fleet;
With England's great Navy he delivered defeat.
Felled by a single shot from a sniper's gun,
He lay dying – his duty done.

'England expects!' he famously cried.
He died with dignity, courage and pride.
His crew returned home our hero in wine,
And laid him in state so we could stand in line.
Lay in peace, Lord Nelson,
With Collingwood at your side,
As we direct to you, our national pride.

The dome is a landmark with its cross and ball,
It stood defiantly through it all.
A blitz of red fell from planes high above,
With intent to destroy the London we love.

Churchill beseeched St Paul's Fire Watch,
'Save the cathedral at any cost'.
The bravery of those led by Matthews and Allen,
Secured the cathedral's future into the new millennium.

Scattered above and well below ground,
Chapels of prayer can be found:
St Dunstan's, All Souls, the OBE,
Lord Kitchener lying solemnly.

The Diehard Regiment remembers battles past,
Mourning those friends and colleagues lost.
The American chapel so bright and so new,
Reminds us of the pain that nation went through.
Twenty-eight thousand American dead,
Recorded in a book,
Bound in blood red.

The high altar nearby commemorates the commonwealth dead,
Two global conflicts of war; another we dread.
The crypt, once a place only for the dead,
Is now brightly lit, to baptise and wed.

The ghosts of artists of the Royal Academy,
Converse with musicians – surreptitiously.
Alexander Fleming is honoured, Cripps the same,
Among many other well-known names.
Wellington and Nelson take pride of place,
Separated by Our Lady of Grace.

Wren's cathedral of St Paul's built of Portland stone,
Stands tall and resplendent on its own.
A place of Christian worship since 604,
We hope will stand for evermore.

A Relationship That Hasn't Always Been So Special

It was he, who made the Americans cross,
His name: Major General Robert Ross.
Sent to America during the 1812 war,
In which he was ordered to settle a score.

As he razed the White House to the ground,
Hero status in Britain he immediately found.
Those Americans soon evened the score,
When a sniper shot him during the Battle of Baltimore.
These facts a historian duly records,
Upon a stone memorial in St Paul's.

The day before I started on my new team at St Paul's Cathedral in April 2014, my dear mum, Mary, died in her nursing home. She'd suffered with Parkinson's disease for over ten years. It was quite strange; I'm not a particularly religious person, but being at St Paul's a few days after her passing and listening to the Lord's Prayer was very comforting. Karen and I attended the All Souls' Day service later in the year which commemorates those who have departed.

Mum

It has been ten long years since she left us all,
Having answered her maker's call.
She was to us – her three sons –
A loving mother, second to none.

As a mother she was strict and very fair,
Step out of line – we wouldn't dare.
She taught us manners and respect for all,
She was always there when we took a fall.

She guided us through the early years,
The night she passed we shed some tears.
Her job done, she rests in peace,
Our love for her will never cease.

She has five great-grandchildren she never met,
With their births our family's future is set.
They are lively, young and full of go,
Sadly, she is a great-grandmother they will never know.

It's moments like losing a parent that puts everything you have into perspective. Although she had been ill for a number of years, the shock of losing her was very profound. There have been several occasions in my life that, when recalled, make you realise how unstable and insecure our life can be. It could just take a simple set of circumstances to go from a secure, happy home to losing everything: financial security, home and even life. I was deeply saddened at the death of a former colleague some years ago who appeared to have everything in front of him: a loving wife, financial security and a glittering career. He ended his life in the most violent of ways.

A few years ago, I presented a talk on my *Square London* book at a library in the East End of London. A few people turned up, and the talk was well received by an eclectic audience. One elderly gentleman, dressed in a dirty suit with stains on his shirt and tie, came up to me after the talk. He spoke of some bad times that he had experienced recently, capped off with the loss of his beloved wife a few years earlier. He was obviously an educated man and asked what I used to do for a living. This opened the door a little for me to ask some questions, not wishing to pry too deeply. He told me that he used to be a professor of science at the University of Cambridge and started to talk about quantum physics. He now lived on his own in a council flat and, it would appear, was having trouble looking after himself. I think, in reality, he had just given up on life and the once weekly visit to the library was all he had to look forward to. I often think of him, and the experience makes me thankful for what I have.

Thankful

I see him sitting there every day,
Warmed by a blanket that's a dirty grey.
Unclean hair hides the hidden face,
Of a human being, cast off and displaced.

Invisible to the passing hoards,
He reaches out a cupped hand, hoping for reward.
His dirty fingers, a half-eaten stale cake,
Tells me that he's definitely no fake.

He is a father, brother, uncle or son,
A home, a job, he has none.
I approach him with a little fear,
Thankful it's not me sitting there.
I tentatively ask him what help I can give,
He looks at me with no will to live.

He glances past me with a worried eye,
A policeman walks closely by.
Although the idea of arrest to us would be hell,
It would at least provide him with a hot meal and a dry cell.

I enter a cafe and purchase a tea,
I return, hoping he will accept it from me.
With shaking hands, he grasps the cup,
With mournful eyes, he glances up,
A subtle change of expression, the simplest of smiles,
We are kindred spirits for just a while.

I look out for him every day,
There is so much more I wish to say.
I wonder if I could've done any more,
It is something I really wanted to explore.

I travel home to my beautiful wife,
Hoping he has found a safer and more purposeful life.
There, but for the grace of God, go I,
Comforted by the fact I'm not such a tough guy.

September is a busy month for our family. My wife and eldest granddaughter Caoimhe share the same birthday, followed by my youngest daughter Nicola. Invariably, it offers up some of the best weather we enjoy in the UK. It is a time, here in Norfolk, to enjoy the wonders of autumn: big blue skies, the smell of bonfires and the peacefulness of the town getting back to normal following another busy tourist season.

September

Ah! September,
With its weather to remember.
A time when Mother Nature reclaims her bountiful summer gifts,
And pushes us towards the winter shift.

The nights draw in, minutes at a time,
The sunsets, well, they are just sublime.
The leaves on the trees turn from green to golden red,
As we retire ever earlier to the warmth of our beds.

As September rolls into the first of October's storms,
Our memories of summer past will keep us warm.
We hunker down against the cold northerly blasts,
And look forward again to the smell of freshly mown grass.

After twenty-two years living in Martley Drive, Gants Hill, we decided to move to North Norfolk in 2016. Since 1997, we have holidayed in Sheringham. When the children were younger, it was – coupled with the generosity of friends – the only place we could afford. We were always looking at the prices of property every time we came up, with the dream of one day retiring here. The children had all long gone and made lives for themselves, so we decided to sell up. We found the perfect house in Sheringham on the North Norfolk coast (the only house we looked at). The retirement aspect never really worked out, and both of us have continued to work in various jobs. The county of Norfolk is beautiful, the North Norfolk coast stunning. The only real difference we noticed from London was of course the convenience of everything, from doctors to hospitals, frequency of trains and the road systems. It is all part of the attraction, of course, but Norfolk's roads can be frustrating. The county has no motorways.

Let the Train Take the Strain

There are no motorways in Norfolk – that's quite sad;
However, the way people drive up here I'm really rather glad.
There is no average driver; it's either very slow or very fast,
Add the tractors and combine harvesters, it's almost impossible to pass.

Records say there are more rural deaths than in any major town,
The antics of idiots can turn your pants a chocolate brown.
You'll never see a traffic cop unless you are driving at thirty-one,
When out they'll pop from behind a tree, pointing a speed gun.

Every year we dutifully pay our road fund tax,
Yet the council, in relation to potholes, are really rather lax.
During the holiday season, our roads are full and clogged,
With our small seaside towns taken over by visiting mobs.

The council love roadworks and a random traffic light,
Sometimes every few miles – you get sick of the sight.
If you decide to visit our county, take the train,
It's good for your mental health – and less of a strain.

After I retired, I started to do some work in the private sector around railway security. Again, it involved travelling away from home but not on such a regular basis. I was self-employed and dreaded the end of January: completion of my tax return. I did honestly, one year, totally mess it up, which brought the attention of HMRC to my door.

The Taxman (or Woman)

Sorting through all the junk mail and tat,
I came across something menacing on my doormat,
An embossed brown envelope from HMRC.
I turned it over tentatively,
Hoping it was addressed to my wife – not me!

You can imagine my genuine shock,
Informing me that I was under investigation and may end up in the dock.
When my heart rate returned to under a hundred,
I tried to work out where I'd blundered.

I collapsed on the sofa – I needed a drink,
And required more time to consider and think.
I grabbed a glass and a bottle of wine,
Then I realised it was only ten past nine.

They calculated that I owed them two grand,
What was I to do? I never had that amount in hand.
I called the tax office; a friendly voice answered the phone –
She was sympathetic, interested without ever uttering a sigh or a moan.

I explained where I thought I'd stupidly gone wrong;
She listened carefully while I whined on and on,
Interrupting only with some comforting verbs,
Until I reached the end of my pathetic blurb.

She asked me to hold and played me some soothing Handel,
All I could think of was the impending shame and scandal.
Moments later, she interrupted 'The Messiah',
Initially my predicament seemed pretty dire.

She said, 'We can see quite clearly from the tax form you filled in,
That you made an honest mistake.' I felt really dim.
'I'm satisfied there was no criminal intent,
To steal from or defraud Her Majesty's Government.
This time you get a warning with no extra penalty to pay,
You owe us two grand and have two weeks from today.'

I sat down sweating in my pants and my vest,
A little worried about the pains in my chest,
I've learnt my lesson – never short change HMRC,
Even though my actions were down to a certain naivety.

Take a lesson from me when completing your books,
Get an accountant and keep off their hook.

I still return to London once every two weeks to go to St Paul's Cathedral. It's an early start on the first train out of Sheringham at 6.18am and arriving back at 8pm. I still love the buzz of the city, but I'm always happy to return home. London has changed greatly in the past decade. Changes in the road systems: one-way streets now two-way; large swathes of the city like Bank Junction a no-go area for cars; bicycle lanes everywhere; the congestion charge; and the latest scheme: the Ultra-Low Emission Zone (ULEZ). It's a war on the motor vehicle – simple as that.

A Drive in London

It used to be such a pleasure,
Driving around London, exploring its treasures.
Travelling across the Thames to and fro,
Waving at people passing below.

Pleasure ships float, lights ablaze,
Happy people enjoying the late summer haze.
A tour guide's voice could be heard to shout,
Pointing at the buildings there about.

Today it is such a shame,
With climate warming there to blame,
That one can no longer afford to explore the sites,
Or experience London, especially at night.

From the comfort of one's car,
We can no longer look afar.
Our politicians have decided,
That the poor motorist should be punished and derided.

Decisions made by various mayors,
In order to clean up London's air,
Have seen the introduction of cycle lanes,
Everywhere, anytime, they are such a pain.

A taxi journey takes twice as long,
Often sitting in a stationary throng.
Buses and bikes have right of way,
What about the poor motorists, some will say.

Oh, how I miss those family times,
Driving past as Big Ben chimes.
Down Cheapside to hear Bow Bells shout,
Motor cars must now stay out!

I must finish with a moan,
What with Khan's Ultra Low Emission Zone,
And around every turning a camera or a cone,
To now drive around London, you a need a personal loan!

Another moan (strange for me as I'm usually a glass-half-full person) is the lack of good old-fashioned cafes in London or, as we used to call them, 'Greasy Spoons'. I know that it's all about healthy living nowadays, but I'd like the choice. On my walk from Liverpool Street station to St Paul's, I pass thirty-three coffee shops of differing names. Most do offer some sort of breakfast items. Normally bacon or sausage rolls, packaged in plastic and microwaved within an inch of their lives. These shops, a little like our American friends, have no idea how to cook bacon. I'm aware of one greasy spoon that has survived the coffee shop/artisan bakery takeover on my route to St Paul's, but it is always *full* (now there's a clue).

We are blessed in Sheringham where we still have a couple of greasy spoons in which one can order a decent full English breakfast: The Kitchen is my choice should you ever visit us here in this beautiful town; although, proprietors of The Kitchen – Jackie and Jim – would probably be slightly aggrieved at being described as such. I should point out that the next poem is *not* a description of their fine establishment.

The Greasy Spoon

A bacon sandwich and a builder's tea,
In a greasy spoon, quite near to me.
Windows misted, plastic seats,
Chalked upon a board – a list to eat.

Chips with everything is the owner's mantra,
If you smile at the waitress – even a Fanta.
Healthy options – should you ask,
Are met with a contemptuous smile and a perfunctory glance.

Red and brown are a must,
In HP and Heinz we as a nation trust.
One in a glass bottle served with a flow,
The other squeezed from a large plastic tomato.

After a full English served on a sea of greasy fat,
I'm summoned into my doctor's surgery for a serious chat.
'Your belly is expanding,' he says to me,
'Your arteries are blocked,
It's time to sit down and take stock.'

He puts me on some scales,
And sticks a needle in my arm,
Before sitting down in a chair and looking at me with an indignant calm.

I can't abide coffee or fancy cakes,
When a barista offered me a latte and some sort of bake,
I nearly had a heart attack at the price it costs to make.

I still occasionally go back to the greasy spoon,
Between trips to the gym.
The alternative is six feet under in a wooden box,
With people singing depressing hymns.

Sheringham is generally a peaceful place. Yet, in the summer season, it can get a little lively. When I was serving in uniform in London, one of the worst situations to be called to was a disturbance involving the fairer sex. As a police officer, you were faced with a lose-lose situation. Although the violence could be extreme, you could not be seen to be too heavy-handed as these were *only* women, tearing lumps out of each other.

Two Ladies Fighting

Can there be a more savage sight,
Than two ladies having a rare old fight?
As they snarl and spit, gouge and bite,
Defending themselves with all their might.

Egged on by a crowd who've gathered around,
Cheering and booing raising the sound.
Violent blows land with a groan and a thud,
The audience applaud at the first sight of blood.

A man whose attention the combatants seek,
Looks embarrassed, mild-mannered and very meek.
He turns away, having no wish to stay,
He has no interest in witnessing this violent affray.

Both ladies have a handful of hair,
In the art of street fighting, they show some flair.
They pull and tug with violent intent,
Until both collapsing, exhausted and spent.

They straighten their clothes, exhibiting no shame,
Looking around for the cheat who is partly to blame.
The spectacle over with, the crowd disappears,
The ladies return back inside to consume more beer.

Events such as street fights are thankfully very rare in our little town. We have half a dozen or so pubs that, in winter, are very quiet. As with most of the country, the traditional pub is disappearing at a worryingly fast rate. Many pubs now promote food above the traditional ale and have become more like restaurants, allowing screaming kids to run around unchallenged with parents who do not seem to notice or care.

My Local

I'm sat in a pub called the Robin Hood,
Is it time to go? I know I should.
I rarely partake on my own,
As I like to drink whilst having a moan.

World politics, the economy, the NHS,
Are all subjects we like to test.
Football always raises the blood pressure hither,
Which we usually lower by discussing the weather.

The pub is in a seaside town,
Another nearby is called the Crown.
In the summer we get taken over,
From people all over; including Dover.

The food is good, the pub very clean,
But when it comes to a lock-in, they can be a bit mean.
In the winter months a fire roars,
As the North Sea wind rattles the doors.
With good real ale available to sup,
I think I'll stay until drinking time's up.

When the holidaymakers arrive, the town's population can double or triple in size, not just humans but canines. The town's pavements are not the widest, and it becomes quite difficult to navigate around a person who has several dogs in tow. Most dog owners are responsible people – some not.

Man's Best Friend

What can we non-dog owners do,
To clean our streets of canine poo?
Maybe we could introduce a cleaning tax,
For those irresponsible owners who are so very lax.

It is unacceptable in law for us humans to beg,
But a dog can walk anywhere and cock a leg.
Unaware of the mess it makes,
As it squats on all fours and defecates,
In full view of those who make to pass,
If we're lucky it would've found some grass.

Once having completed its dirty task,
And shaking its bum to remove the last,
It looks around in a spin,
Grinning at its owner, who's searching for a bin.
A black poo bag now in tow,
Happily, a discovery of a bush in which to throw.

They have to go – we know that's true,
But responsible owners surely agree,
We must keep our streets and parks dog poo free.

There is no doubt holidaymakers bring much-needed cash into the town. Without visitors, many of our small, independent businesses would not survive the winter months. The national trend of closing banks, especially in rural areas, has had a profound effect in North Norfolk. When writing this (October 2023), we have only one bank and one building society remaining in the town. Cromer has two banks and Holt none at all. It's a normal state of affairs for ATMs to run out of cash by mid-morning on a weekday and the same on a Saturday morning.

There's a Bank – Where?

Can anybody remember – and let's be frank –
When you could set off and walk to your local bank?
A friendly face sat behind some glass,
With whom you could discuss times gone past.

Lots of pamphlets on display,
Information on loans and how much to pay.
Mortgage terms and interest rates,
All on show for perusal and debate.
A helpful member of banking staff,
Would often approach with a smile and share a laugh.

Lines of ATMs where you could draw your hard-earned cash,
And supplement your dwindling stash.
'Cash is King' they used to say,
Now a card and bleep is the modern way to pay.

Lloyds, NatWest, Barclays too,
Have all disappeared from our view.
From town to town we have to hop,
And all we find are charity shops.

Another British tradition falls away,
Banking CEOs we must thank,
For the demise and death of our local bank.

One of the reasons I travel down to St Paul's from North Norfolk is to meet up with a bunch of people whom I regard as good friends. Some of them I have known for ten years or more. Sadly, over the years, we have lost several of them. One such person was Tom. He was a man I greatly respected. A charismatic figure to not only me personally but also to the rest of the team and all the visitors he would guide around the cathedral in his own inimitable style.

A True English Gent

His name was Tom, a true English gent,
Who earnt one's respect wherever he went.
He told stories we'd all heard before,
But always we listened, eager for more.

He wore his red sash with ornate pride,
As he patrolled the cathedral floor with a purposeful stride,
From under the dome to the transepts and aisles,
Chattering with tourists, making them smile.

One day when again Great Paul rings from high above,
We know he'll be looking down – brimming with love.
His name was Tom, a true English gent,
Who earnt one's respect wherever he went.

I enjoy the company of all those on the Wednesday team at St Paul's. My cathedral guiding badge, along with my police long service and good conduct medal, are my most prized personal possessions. As we lose members to the passage of time or illness, we thankfully have new members regularly joining us adding energy and enthusiasm. One particular lady makes me laugh constantly. She can convey her mood and what she is thinking with a single look or a glance.

That's a Ripper

I know a girl of Aussie birth,
She originates from the other side of Earth.
For sure her heart is still at home,
But she's been here so long, she's a full-blown pom.

She tells jokes you've probably heard,
And takes her name from our national bird.
She is a fun-loving soul and part of the Wednesday crew,
And doesn't remotely smell like a kangaroo.

She has a steely side, cross her if you dare,
When upset by certain people, she can produce a scary stare.
Pleasingly, she doesn't call everybody 'mate',
One of us poms' Aussie pet hates.
She never calls out 'that's a ripper',
And is slightly too old to be a stripper.

I've known her for a little over a year,
If she wasn't teetotal, we'd probably enjoy a beer.
We are both of an age where tolerance wears thin,
And no longer enjoy wrinkle-free skin.

She enjoys a little gossip and a juicy rumour,
And understands succinctly my wicked sense of humour.
At an age where a shower is preferable to a bath,
Thank God we can still enjoy a ruddy good laugh.

We are lucky enough to have lovely front and rear gardens surrounding our house in Sheringham. Neither Karen nor I were gardeners before we moved here; mowing the grass was about my limit. But we took on the gardens with vigour and enthusiasm with the help of a very knowledgeable gardener. In pride of place are the hydrangeas at the front which I will not let anybody touch – they are my pride and joy. For the last couple of summers, we have noticed, on occasions, a terrible smell. I first thought it was a hedgehog or a rat that had died behind the shed. Eventually, we discovered the source of the smell: a stinkhorn mushroom.

The Shameless Phallus

It smells of death and rotting flesh,
Standing proud and erect it appears afresh.
Without notice it emerges from the ground,
This is where the stinkhorn mushroom can be found.

It can grow as much as twenty-five centimetres tall,
And usually makes its appearance when leaves turn to red and fall.
Phallus Impudicus is its botanical name,
If you can't smell your roses, then it's to blame.

It oozes a spore-bearing sticky gel;
It attracts the flies, and it stinks like hell.
The cap is coated in a sticky green slime;
Thankfully, it often disappears in quick time.

There have been some imaginative names over the years,
One of these may cause you a shock,
It was known in parts of our land as dead man's…
Oh dear, it seems I've developed somewhat of a mental block.

I've always been very proud of my nationality. We Brits have our faults but must be the most tolerant nation on Earth. I believe that a United Kingdom will always be stronger together.

Us British

Us British, we are a simple folk,
Our sense of humour is often poked.
However, wind us up the wrong way –
As our enemies have found – you will pay.

We take our traditions to the extreme,
We like our strawberries covered in cream.
We invented most modern sports,
Cricket, football and all other sorts.

We love to think outside the box,
With brains like Hawking and Brian Cox.
We gave the world Shakespearean plays,
Fingerprints and DNA.

We are an island nation as you know,
We often get covered in ice and snow.
Our weather is traditionally wet;
However, it's not the thing on which you would bet.

The French say they hate our food,
The Italians, that we are a grumpy brood.
When it comes to favouring matt or gloss,
As with all things, we don't give a toss.

We are a generous people, some may say,
We work hard for our money and know how to play.
But billions are handed by our governmental buffoons,
To India and China so they can land on the moon.

We haven't been invaded for a thousand years,
Hitler's efforts would end in tears.
But here we are allowing men of fighting age,
To stay in our country without earning a wage.
We put them in hotels and give them some dough,
We have no idea if they are friend or foe.

We are, without doubt, the greatest country on Earth,
A place of free speech where you can spout your pennies worth.
We have our problems which we cannot swerve,
But confront them with countless energy and verve,
A tiny island surrounded by the sea,
In which our children can grow and be free.

As a proud Englishman, I do think we get the thin end of the unified wedge. We have given the other three nations the ability to govern themselves, yet the interests of England are often forgotten. This is emphasised in the national anthem, when the United Kingdom is collectively represented. Such as at the Olympic Games, when the national anthem is sung. However, when the four countries compete as separate nations such as in football and rugby to mention a few, Scotland, Wales and Northern Ireland revert to a national song; us English continue to use the national anthem. This often leads to the distasteful booing of our national anthem when sung by an English team.

The English National Anthem

'God save the King',
We proudly pronounce,
As we stand side by side,
Four countries, united, singing with pride.

As at the Olympics for Team GB, we rise from our seats,
We honour this United Kingdom and its incredible feats.
Although we are tolerant and offer a welcome to all,
Our national anthem is our collective call.

However, the Scots celebrate, when representing their own,
Demanding the English King immediately returns home.
The Welsh sing of the land of their fathers with their Celtic passion laid bare,
Whilst the people of Northern Ireland take in Londonderry's Air.

Yet when an England team stands in line with chests puffed out,
When our close neighbours deem fit to both vilify and shout,
Surely it is now time for us English to proclaim,
Lyrics of our own on which to light our passionate flame.

Blake's poem about England's mountains green,
Adapted by Parry to music and an orchestral theme,
Gives proud reverence to the English way of life, which many deride,
Let the words of 'Jerusalem' be sung high and wide.

I am now fully immersed in Norfolk life. I love the clean air, the big skies and the laid-back attitude to life. As I reach my mid-sixties, I have become much more contemplative about life in general. We have five grandchildren: Caoimhe, Albie, Callan, Olivia and Mason, whom we both adore. I take in much more of my surroundings now, than when working and raising a family, and record many of the people I meet and occasions in verse.

The Local Council

Whether they be green, red, blue or yellow,
Some will have loud, opinionated voices, others more mellow.
The town clerk gets paid a fair old whack,
To keep the councillors in line and on track.

They have a full meeting once a month or so,
When council taxpayers can come to and fro.
Many subjects are discussed about when, how and where,
Accompanied by a lot of hot air.

A big responsibility – millions of pounds to spend,
Decisions – on which political loyalties and opinions depend.
The meetings can be heated, and tempers tend to flare,
Over projects and plans on which they care.

When suggesting policies, they must make a careful selection,
As in four years' time, they'll be up for re-election.
However, they give up their time without any pay,
To make our lives run smoothly from day to day.

Cows in a Field

I saw some cows in a field,
To be honest, they looked pretty chilled.
Their udders swung from left to right,
Full of milk – they looked pretty tight.

They chew and chew on so much grass,
The resulting air has to pass,
It rises way, way into the sky,
Making environmentalists sob and cry.

To be milked, they form an orderly line,
As they munch away – life is fine.
The milking machine vibrates and starts,
Don't stand behind one, as they are prone to fart.

Once relieved of their precious load,
They stroll back out and once again adopt a chilled mode.
I'd love to be a cow,
Enjoying life to the full,
Until the farmer opens the gate,
And lets in a rampant bull.

The Granny Flat

It seemed such a good idea at the time,
From then on it turned into a pantomime.
The builders said it would be a six-week job,
They'd have it done before winter – no prob.

Winter came and winter went,
Hours and hours on the phone we spent.
Just as the Easter bunnies started to hop,
The building work – at last it stopped.

Our garage now turned into a granny flat,
When Mother-In-Law arrived we had a spat.
I've never seen so much stuff,
The skip we'd hired wasn't big enough.

Why did she need two dozen cup-a-soups?
Scores of pickles and spaghetti hoops.
I started to rant and got the hump,
Followed by frequent trips to the council dump.

Now settled in with her yappy dog,
Life for her is not such a slog.
We hope some happiness she will find,
And it's given my wife some peace of mind.

The Bowling Green

Is there anything more serene,
Than spending a few hours on the bowling green?
It is a very simple game,
All you need is a relatively good aim.
You roll your wood, whilst taking care of your back,
And try and finish alongside that little white jack.

Scores are kept, points accrued,
Then it's back to the clubhouse for a few jars and some food.
Quintessentially so English, on a surface so grand,
Competitors chat and shake each other's hands.
There is no animosity or the settling of scores,
The next friendly match is arranged before heading for the doors.

It is such a pleasant sight to see,
Human beings getting along so amicably.
No fighting, swearing, angst or bull,
Just a group of people living life to the full.

The Future

For those of a certain age,
For whom reading a book still means turning a page.
Who will remember when men proudly wore ties,
And people passing each other stopped and said 'Hi'.

Remember when we could have a laugh and even take the mick,
All we hear now is it's either 'woke' or 'sick'.
When a soap opera appeared just once a week,
With violent-free storylines and no knife-wielding freaks.

Remember the times when children could read and spell,
Recite dates and places of historical battles as well.
Nowadays, many of the do-gooder class want to condemn our history to the past,
It's up to us oldies to stand up and shout,
We must defend our national heroes no doubt.

The older we get, the more remote we feel,
Modern life takes over – nothing seems real.
Scammers and AI, whatever next,
I struggle to put it all into some context.

I'm not sure where life goes from here,
I suppose keep things simple and live out my years.
The love and well-being my family bring,
Makes the future not such a frightening thing.